We all live under the same sky

Auntie, you and I

We acknowledge the Traditional Owners of the land on which our book is based. We pay our respects to their Elders, past and present, and the Aboriginal Elders of other communities who may be here today.

My Auntie Lives in Australia

It's very far away
But I love her very much
And I miss her every day

Dedicated to Jimi, the little one who inspired this book

My Auntie lives in Australia

It's very far away

She told me about the kangaroos

Hooray Hooray Hooray!

Kangaroos have big tails to help them balance when they - **BOUNCE!**

Mummy kangaroos keep their baby safe in a pouch.

A baby kangaroo is called a Joey!

My Auntie lives in Australia

It's very far away

She told me about the Great Barrier Reef

Hooray Hooray Hooray!

The Great Barrier Reef is made up of lots and LOTS of coral. Coral is an **animal**, not a plant.

Over 9000 species live there! It is so **BIG** that it can be seen from outer space!

"Has your Auntie visited the reef?"

My Auntie lives in Australia

It's very far away

She told me about Australia Zoo

Hooray Hooray Hooray!

Australia Zoo is a world famous wildlife park in Queensland (the Sunshine State).

It has the **LARGEST wildlife hospital in the world** where it cares for sick, injured and orphaned native wildlife until they are well enough to return to the wild!

My Auntie lives in Australia

It's very far away

She told me about Uluru

Hooray Hooray Hooray!

Uluru is a really, *REALLY* **BIG** rock in the middle of Australia.

It is brown but when the sun shines on it, Uluru looks bright red!
Uluru is **550 MILLION** years old. That's *VERY* old!

"*Would you like to travel to the "Red Centre" with your Auntie one day?*"

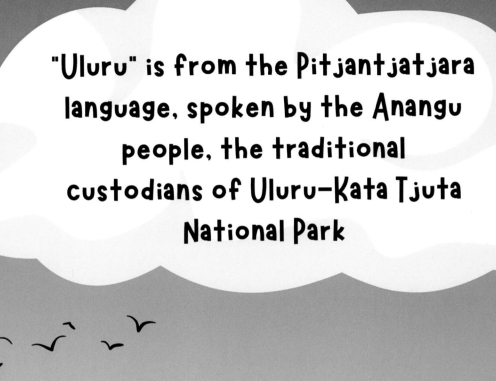

"Uluru" is from the Pitjantjatjara language, spoken by the Anangu people, the traditional custodians of Uluru-Kata Tjuta National Park

My Auntie lives in Australia

It's very far away

She told me about the platypus

Hooray Hooray Hooray!

With the bill and feet of a duck, the body of an otter, and the tail of a beaver, the **platypus** looks so strange that some people used to think they were fake!

You can ONLY find platypuses in Australia, where they live in freshwater rivers and burrow to lay eggs - very unusual for a mammal!

My Auntie lives in Australia

It's very far away

She told me about boomerangs

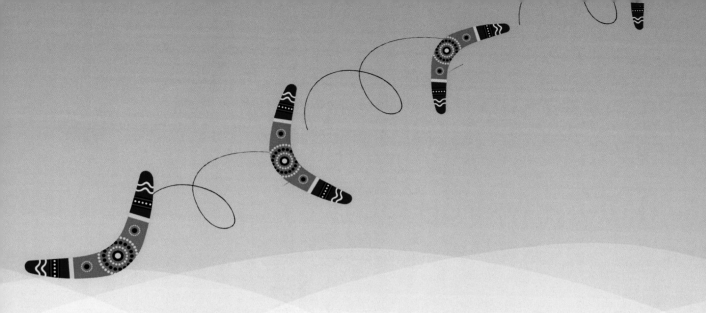

Hooray Hooray Hooray!

Boomerangs are throwing sticks - some even return to the thrower! WATCH OUT!

The Aboriginal Peoples of Australia used boomerangs for hunting. Indigenous Australian paintings show boomerangs being used over 50,000 years ago! That's a LOOONG time!

"Indigenous" people means people who lived in the country first!

Today boomerangs are used mostly for fun!
Does your Auntie play with boomerangs?

My Auntie lives in Australia

It's very far away

She told me about surfing

Hooray Hooray Hooray!

BEWARE

OF SHARKS

Surfing is a FUN water activity where you ride waves by standing or lying down on a surfboard.

Australians love to surf because it has LOTS of beaches with BIG waves!

"Just tell your Auntie to watch out for..."

My Auntie lives in Australia

It's very far away

She told me about the creepy

crawlies & critters

Hooray Hooray Hooray!

hisssss

UH OH, there are lots of **creepy crawlies and critters** in Australia...

But even though they look a bit scary, they are just part of nature and won't bother us if we don't bother them.

Instead of being scared of them, why don't we learn about them instead?

"Ask your Auntie more about creepy crawlies."

My Auntie lives in Australia

It's very far away

She told me about the Sydney Opera

House

Hooray Hooray Hooray!

The **Sydney Opera House** is a famous building on the shores of Sydney Harbour.

It is **shaped like the sails of a boat.**

Many concerts and BIG events take place there all year round!

My Auntie lives in Australia

It's very far away

She told me about barbecues

Hooray Hooray Hooray!

When the weather is warm and sunny, Australians love to make food on the "*barbie*".

You can cook meat, seafood and vegetables on the barbecue. ***YUM!***

The BEST way to have a barbecue is to invite friends over, share food and have FUN!

My Auntie lives in Australia

It's very far away

SHE TOLD ME HOW MUCH SHE LOVES ME

Hooray Hooray Hooray!

www.childrensbookstobondover.com
@childrensbookstobondover

Manufactured by Amazon.com.au
Sydney, New South Wales, Australia